Published in 2014 by The Rosen Publishing Group, Inc.
29 East 21st Street, New York, NY 10010

Photo Credits: **KEY** tl=top left; tc=top center; tr=top right; cl=center left; c=center; cr=center right; b=bottom; bl=bottom left; bc=bottom center; br=bottom right; bg=background

CBT = Corbis; GI = Getty Images; iS = istockphoto.com; RH = Random House; SH = Shutterstock; TF = Topfoto; wiki = Wikipedia

2tc TF; **3**bg iS; c, tl, tr TF; **8**br, cl TF; tr wiki; **9**bg iS; cl, cr TF; **10**bl TF; **10–11**bg iS; **14**br GI; c TF; **15**bg GI; **16**bc, tl TF; **16–17**bg iS; **17**tl, tr TF; **18**bc, cr TF; **19**bg TF; **20**tr CBT; tr GI; **20–21**bg CBT; **21**tr CBT; tr TF; **22**tl TF; **23**b, tc TF; **24**cr TF; **24–25**bg iS; **25**br, c iS; cl, cr, tl TF; **26–27**bg iS; **27**br iS; **28**bl, br, br, c, tr iS; bl SH; br, cl TF; **29**bl, br, tl, tr iS; b, c, cr, tl, tr TF; **30**c, cr TF; **32**bg iS

All illustrations copyright Weldon Owen Pty Ltd. **6**bl, **22**bl Andrew Davies/Creative Communication; **26–27** Peter Bull Art Studio

Weldon Owen Pty Ltd
Managing Director: Kay Scarlett
Creative Director: Sue Burk
Publisher: Helen Bateman
Senior Vice President, International Sales: Stuart Laurence
Vice President Sales North America: Ellen Towell
Administration Manager, International Sales: Kristine Ravn

Library of Congress Cataloging-in-Publication Data

Brasch, Nicolas.
  Leonardo da Vinci : the greatest inventor / By Nicolas Brasch.
      pages cm. — (Discovery education : discoveries and inventions)
  Includes index.
  ISBN 978-1-4777-1330-3 (library binding) — ISBN 978-1-4777-1502-4 (pbk.) —
ISBN 978-1-4777-1503-1 (6-pack)
  1. Leonardo, da Vinci, 1452–1519—Juvenile literature. 2. Scientists—Italy—Biography—Juvenile literature. 3. Artists—Italy—Biography—Juvenile literature. I. Title.
  Q143.L5B73 2014
  709.2—dc23
  [B]
                                    2012043620

Manufactured in the United States of America

CPSIA Compliance Information: Batch #S13PK3: For Further Information contact Rosen Publishing, New York, New York at 1-800-237-9932

LEONARDO DA VINCI
THE GREATEST INVENTOR

NICOLAS BRASCH

PowerKiDS press.

New York

Contents

Who Was Leonardo?

Leonardo da Vinci was a man ahead of his time. He was a genius: a brilliant artist, as well as an inventor, architect, scientist, engineer, and much more. Leonardo lived at the start of a period known as the Renaissance. This was a time when great art was produced, significant scientific discoveries were made, and important ideas were discussed.

Italy is in Central Europe.

Leonardo's birthplace
Leonardo da Vinci was born on April 15, 1452 near the village of Vinci, near Florence in northern Italy.

1452–1519

1452
Leonardo da Vinci is born.

1455
Johannes Gutenberg uses a printing press to print the Bible.

1462
Ivan the Great becomes leader of Russia.

1485
The War of the Roses ends in England.

1492
Christopher Columbus sets sail from Spain on the *Santa Maria*, landing in the Americas in October that year.

1497
Vasco da Gama leaves Portugal to sail to India via the Cape of Good Hope.

1504
Michelangelo sculpts the statue of David.

1509
Henry VIII becomes king of England.

1517
Martin Luther, a German scholar, publishes 95 objections to Catholic practices.

1519
Explorer Ferdinand Magellan sets out to circumnavigate the globe. Leonardo da Vinci dies.

Self-portrait?
Art historians argue whether or not Leonardo ever drew a portrait of himself. This is a copy of a famous red chalk drawing allegedly drawn by Leonardo when he was about sixty years old, although he looks older.

Fact or Fiction?
Leonardo da Vinci was a perfectionist. Before he died he was believed to have said, "I have offended God and mankind because my work did not reach the quality it should have."

Young Leonardo

When Leonardo da Vinci was born, his father and mother were not married. Leonardo lived with his mother until he was five, then with his father's family. He eventually had 12 stepbrothers and stepsisters, although he remained a loner.

Casa Leonardo
The house where Leonardo is believed to have grown up is 2 miles (3 km) north of Vinci.

First work
Leonardo's earliest known artwork is a pen and ink drawing of the Arno River, near where he lived. It is believed to have been drawn on August 5, 1473.

Baptism of Christ
Leonardo worked with several artists, including his master, Verrocchio, on the *Baptism of Christ*, completed in 1475. Some reports claim that Leonardo's work on the young, kneeling angel was so good that Verrocchio gave up painting.

Leonardo the apprentice

Leonardo da Vinci began his professional career working in the workshop of the artist Verrocchio. Verrocchio was a sculptor, goldsmith, and painter who was considered Florence's greatest artist at that time. Many artists worked at Verrocchio's workshop, which was a center for the training of young artists in Florence. Just to be accepted as an apprentice into the workshop was an indication that a young artist had talent.

Tobias and the Angel

Tobias and the Angel is a work that came from Verrocchio's workshop. Some art historians believe that Leonardo painted the fish and the dog.

❝ *Knowing is not enough; we must apply. Being willing is not enough; we must do.* ❞

LEONARDO DA VINCI

The young David

One of Verrocchio's greatest works is a bronze statue of David with the head of Goliath placed at his feet. Some art historians believe Leonardo modeled for this statue.

Machines of War

Leonardo da Vinci was constantly using his imagination to come up with ideas for new modes of transportation and war machines. His drawings of war machines were done to impress his patron, Ludovico Sforza, the Duke of Milan. These machines and contraptions were not built in Leonardo's time.

Helicopter
A model of Leonardo's drawing of a flying machine shows it had wings that spun around, like the rotors of a modern helicopter.

Most Illustrious Lord,
Having now sufficiently seen and considered the proofs of all those who count themselves masters and inventors in the instruments of war, and finding that their invention and use does not differ in any respect from those in common practice, I am emboldened ... to put myself in communication with your Excellency, in order to acquaint you with my secrets. ... I offer myself as ready to make a trial of them in whatever place shall please your Excellency, to whom I commend myself with all possible humility.

Impressing the Duke
Leonardo da Vinci wrote a letter to Ludovico Sforza, the Duke of Milan, asking that the Duke consider his ideas for war machines.

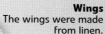

Wings
The wings were made
from linen.

Cannon
Leonardo invented a cannon
that was light and easy to
move on the battlefield.

Aerial screw
An aerial screw turned
as the machine rose
into the air.

Crew
The tank was
designed to
seat eight men.

Turtle shell
The tank was
shaped like a turtle,
with metal plates
as reinforcement.

Tank
Leonardo told the
Duke of Milan the tank
would be "good for
breaking the ranks,
but you will want to
follow it up."

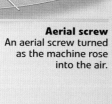

Cannons
Cannons were to be fitted
around the base of the tank.

Backpack mechanism

Pulley

Line

Backpack

Tension
line

Flying machine

The idea of the flying machine was that the pilot would jump from a tall structure and start moving his legs up and down to raise the tension lines attached to his feet. These lines were linked to a pulley system that operated the giant wings.

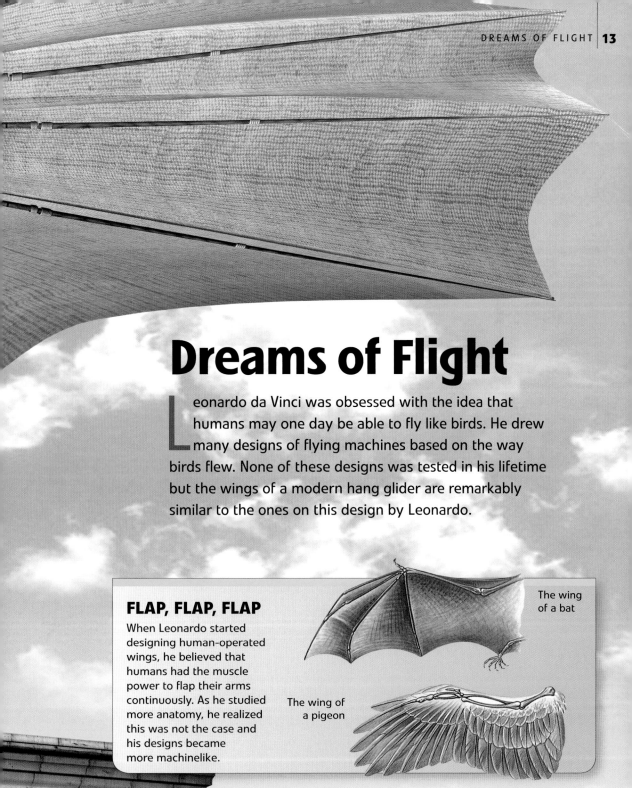

Dreams of Flight

Leonardo da Vinci was obsessed with the idea that humans may one day be able to fly like birds. He drew many designs of flying machines based on the way birds flew. None of these designs was tested in his lifetime but the wings of a modern hang glider are remarkably similar to the ones on this design by Leonardo.

FLAP, FLAP, FLAP

When Leonardo started designing human-operated wings, he believed that humans had the muscle power to flap their arms continuously. As he studied more anatomy, he realized this was not the case and his designs became more machinelike.

The wing of a bat

The wing of a pigeon

Perspective and Proportion

Most of Leonardo's art was very realistic. His interest in perspective and proportion helped him achieve this realism. Perspective is the art of drawing solid objects on a flat surface in such a way that the picture gives the right impression of their size and position, for example, by drawing the more distant objects smaller than closer objects. Leonardo was one of the pioneers of this way of drawing.

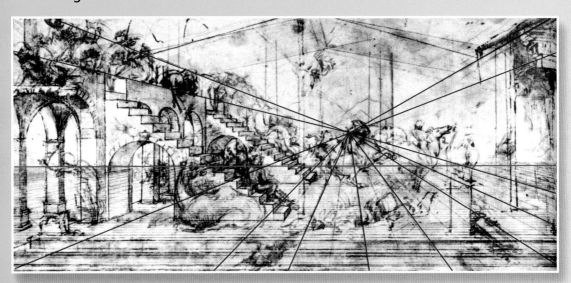

Close to reality
Leonardo's preliminary drawing of *The Adoration of the Magi* (in about 1481) shows that he started by locating a central point (called a vanishing point) for the viewer's eye and then drew the figures and objects behind, in front, or beside this point. Lines are drawn to ensure the artist's final work matches reality as closely as possible.

KEY
—— Horizon line runs along the picture at the viewer's eye level.

—— Orthogonal lines direct the viewer's eye to the vanishing point.

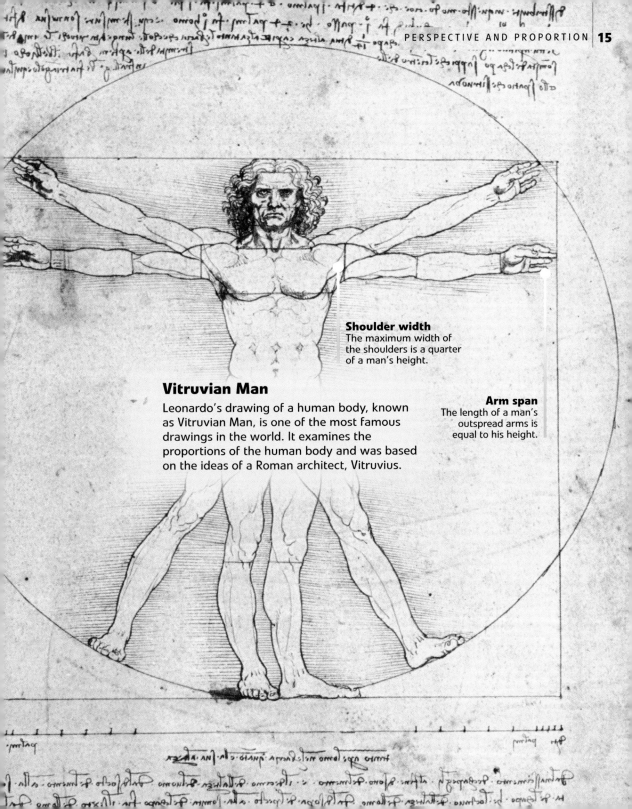

Shoulder width
The maximum width of
the shoulders is a quarter
of a man's height.

Vitruvian Man

Leonardo's drawing of a human body, known
as Vitruvian Man, is one of the most famous
drawings in the world. It examines the
proportions of the human body and was based
on the ideas of a Roman architect, Vitruvius.

Arm span
The length of a man's
outspread arms is
equal to his height.

Anatomy

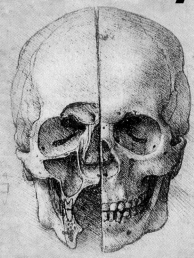

Leonardo da Vinci was fascinated by the human body. He wanted to understand exactly how it worked and how all the pieces fitted together. He did this by cutting open human bodies, mainly those of dead criminals. It was not always easy to get bodies for dissection, because the practice was frowned upon by many people.

Human skull
Leonardo was obsessed with proportion. He was not interested just in the detail of the skull but the relative size of each piece as well.

Body parts
Pen and ink studies of skeletons include details of the human spine, pelvis, and thorax.

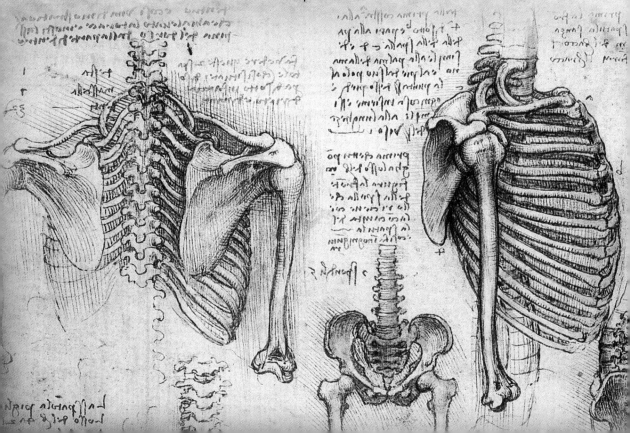

Interesting faces

Leonardo had a fascination with drawing faces. He would memorize an interesting face he had seen and draw it later, capturing the expression perfectly. In the drawings, he demonstrates his knowledge of anatomy, especially in the way he places depressions in parts of the skull.

The lack of refrigeration meant that Leonardo had to examine bodies very quickly, before they started to rot and smell.

Mona Lisa

The *Mona Lisa* is one of the world's most famous paintings, and certainly the most famous portrait. It was painted by Leonardo da Vinci between 1503 and 1506. Among the features that have made it so famous are the way Leonardo used light and shade, as well as placement of the figure in front of a landscape. Also known as *La Gioconda*, *Mona Lisa* hangs in the Louvre, in Paris.

That's Amazing!

Mona Lisa was stolen from the Louvre in 1911 but recovered two years later. However, in those two years, thousands more visitors than usual flocked to the Louvre to see the blank space on the wall.

Smile

Art historians through the ages have tried to figure out what Mona Lisa's faint smile represents. A scientist has revealed that the smile appears bigger when the viewer focuses on the eyes, rather than directly on the mouth.

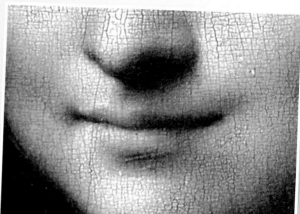

Hands

In Leonardo's time, portraits portrayed their subjects in stiff, upright positions. Mona Lisa is relaxed, as shown by the positioning of her hands.

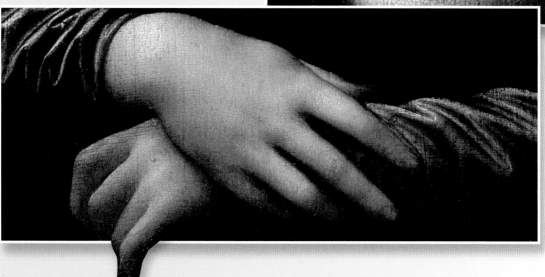

Landscape
The landscape represents Leonardo's fascination with the link between nature and humanity.

Hair
The darkness of Mona Lisa's hair helps to highlight the light of her face and upper body.

Clothes
The folds of Mona Lisa's clothes were created by a painting technique called sfumato. This involves moving from areas of lightness to darkness without lines or borders.

Lisa del Giocondo
For hundreds of years, arguments raged as to who the woman in the portrait was. It is now believed to have been Lisa del Giocondo, wife of a merchant from Florence.

The Last Supper

Leonardo da Vinci's *The Last Supper* is a mural. It was painted between 1495 and 1498 on the back wall of a church in Milan, Italy. Leonardo painted it for his patron Duke Ludovico Sforza. The painting depicts the last supper that Jesus Christ had with his 12 disciples.

RESTORATION

Before   After

Restoration efforts
Leonardo tried a new technique when painting *The Last Supper*. Unfortunately, it did not work and the paint faded. It was restored between 1978 and 1999.

John
John looks as if he is considering Jesus' statement deeply. Some historians have suggested he looks as though he is about to faint.

James
James's reaction to Jesus' statement is one of disbelief and horror.

Judas
Judas looks shocked that Jesus knows what is to come. In his right hand, Judas is clutching the bag of silver he has been paid to betray Jesus.

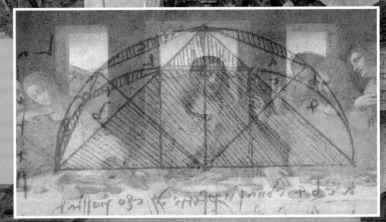

Triangle of stability
Leonardo knew that a triangle represented stability. So apart from placing Jesus in the center of the picture, where the viewer's eye would automatically fall first, he also made sure his image of Jesus formed a triangle.

Jesus Christ
Jesus has just informed his disciples that he knows he is about to be betrayed by one of them.

Thomas
Thomas appears agitated, as if he wants to challenge whoever is going to betray Jesus.

Jude Thaddeus
Jude Thaddeus has turned to Simon as if to figure out what they should do.

Last Years

Leonardo da Vinci lived his last few years in Rome and France. He continued his interest in anatomy, engineering, and the link between nature and humanity right up until his death in France on May 2, 1519.

End of the World
Among Leonardo's last works were a series of 16 small landscapes that he titled *End of the World*. They depict Earth as a violent, furious place.

> **Art is never finished, only abandoned.**
> **LEONARDO DA VINCI**

Where Leonardo lived
Leonardo da Vinci lived in Milan during the period 1482–1500, and again 1506–1513; in Florence 1500–1506; in Rome 1513–1516; and in France from 1516 until his death in 1519.

Last home
Leonardo da Vinci lived his last few years in the castle of Amboise, which stood on a rocky spur above the river Loire in France.

Fact or myth?
This painting depicts King Francis I of France holding Leonardo's head as the artist died. It was based on stories that the king was present at Leonardo's death.

King Francis I
Records show the king was in Germany at the time of Leonardo's death.

Leonardo da Vinci
Leonardo was buried at the castle of Amboise.

?... You Decide

Leonardo da Vinci is considered a genius. Several other figures are also considered geniuses.
You decide who you think is the greatest mind the Western world has ever seen.

Leonardo da Vinci

Born in 1452, Leonardo was best known for his paintings *Mona Lisa* and *The Last Supper* and for his designs of flying machines and other devices.

Leonardo da Vinci

Checklist of Leonardo's skills and talents

- ☑ Introduced new techniques into art.

- ☑ Designed flying machines centuries before they were invented.

- ☑ Designed war machines.

- ☑ Made discoveries about the human body.

- ☑ Painted *Mona Lisa*.

- ☑ Painted *The Last Supper*.

- ☑ Drew the Vitruvian Man.

- ☑ Contributed to the field of engineering.

Newton

Sir Isaac Newton (1643–1727) was a scientist and mathematician who developed the laws of gravity.

❝ *Genius is 1 percent inspiration and 99 percent perspiration.* **❞**
THOMAS EDISON

Einstein

Albert Einstein (1879–1955) was a scientist and mathematician who made many discoveries about time and space.

Mozart

Wolfgang Amadeus Mozart (1756–1791) was a composer and musician who composed more than 600 works.

Other geniuses

Other people considered to be geniuses are Charles Darwin, Michelangelo, Thomas Edison, and Plato. Do some research and find out what they did.

Shakespeare

William Shakespeare (1564–1616) was a writer whose plays include *Romeo and Juliet*, *King Lear*, and *Macbeth*.

How To Send a Secret Mirror Message

Leonardo da Vinci wrote down every idea he ever had. Sadly, only about a quarter of his notebooks have survived through the ages. Leonardo da Vinci wrote most of his notes in mirror writing. For him, it was as natural as writing normally.

2. Write message

Write a word or a sentence on the paper as you normally would.

1. What you need

All you need to write a secret mirror message is some paper, a pen or pencil, and a mirror.

Fact or Fiction?

Some people believe Leonardo used mirror writing because he was left-handed and did not want to smudge the page.

3. Copy message

Place your original message in front of a mirror and then copy the mirror image onto a new piece of paper.

4. Read message

Few people will be able to understand your message unless they know to put it in front of a mirror.

A SECRET MESSAGE

Can you read the message on the right without putting it in front of a mirror?

Come quickly!
I found some
money hidden
in the garden.

Leonardo's Ideas

O ne of the most fascinating things about the ideas that Leonardo da Vinci came up with is that he thought of things hundreds of years before they were actually developed and built. And while many famous figures in history have conceived one or two great ideas, Leonardo proposed dozens of them throughout his lifetime. Here are some familiar inventions.

Helicopter
Leonardo was the first to envisage a helicopter-like machine.

1480s

Helicopter

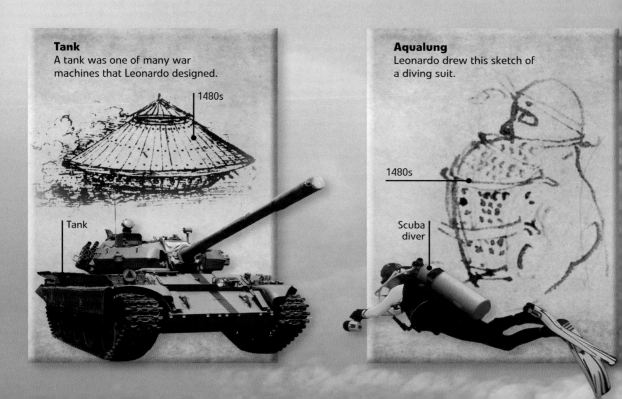

Tank
A tank was one of many war machines that Leonardo designed.

1480s

Tank

Aqualung
Leonardo drew this sketch of a diving suit.

1480s

Scuba diver

Parachute

Leonardo's parachute resembled a tent with handles.

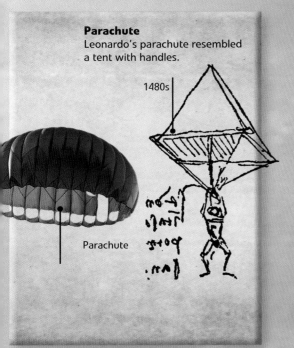

1480s

Parachute

Bicycle

It is unclear whether Leonardo designed the first bicycle or if this sketch is a hoax.

Perhaps 1490s

Racing bicycle

Flying machine

This is just one of many flying machines designed by Leonardo.

1480s

Hang glider

Bridge

A lightweight, movable bridge was designed by Leonardo for military use.

1480s

Arch bridge

Look Into the Future

Now that you have read this book you will know that Leonardo da Vinci drew sketches of many devices that were not invented for hundreds of years. He looked into the future and thought about what humans might need.

Now it is your turn to step into Leonardo's shoes.

Think about what the world will be like in about 400 years.

Then design a device that will help make life better or easier or more exciting for the people living in the year 2400.

Here are some questions to help you with your writing:

1 How will humans be traveling from country to country in 2400?

2 What sort of devices will kitchens have to make it easy to prepare food?

3 What will the classroom of the future look like?

4 What devices will be used to clean the house?

Glossary

acquaint (uh-KWAYNT)
To become familiar with.

anatomy (uh-NA-tuh-mee)
The study of the structure
(body) of animals or plants.

circumnavigate
(SER-kem-NA-vuh-gayt)
To sail completely
around something.

commend (kuh-MEND)
To recommend.

continuously
(kun-TIN-yoo-us-lee)
Without stopping.

contraptions
(kun-TRAP-shunz) Devices.

depict (dih-PIKT)
To show; represent.

genius (JEEN-yus)
Someone who is much
smarter than most people.

horizon line
(huh-RY-zun LYN) A line that
marks the viewer's eye level.

humanity
(hyoo-MA-nuh-tee) Having to
do with humans.

humility
(hyoo-MIH-luh-tee) The
quality of being humble.

illustrious
(ih-LUS-tree-us) Describes
someone or something that is
important, respected,
and famous.

landscape (LAND-skayp)
Scenery.

merchant (MER-chunt)
Seller; trader.

mural (MYUR-ul)
Artwork on a wall or ceiling.

obsession (ahb-SEH-shun)
Fascination.

orthogonal
(or-THAH-guh-nul) Made up
of right angles.

patron (PAY-trun)
Someone who provides
financial support to an artist.

perspective
(per-SPEK-tiv) A way of
drawing a scene so that the
picture gives the right
impression of the size and
position of the objects in it.

preliminary
(prih-LIH-muh-nehr-ee)
Before the main matter.

proportion
(pruh-POR-shun) The size of
something in relation to
something else.

pulley (PU-lee) A device
that makes it easier to move
a rope or chain up and down.

realism (REE-uh-lih-zim)
Like real life.

reinforcement
(ree-in-FORS-ment)
Extra protection.

Renaissance
(REH-nuh-sons) A period
of history from 1400s–1600s
when many discoveries
were made.

scholar (SKAH-ler)
Someone who studies.

stability (stuh-BIH-luh-tee)
Strength; firmness.

thorax (THOR-aks)
The area of the body between
the neck and the lower
chest that contains the lungs
and heart.

vanishing point
(VA-nish-ing POYNT)
The place in a drawing at
which parallel lines seem
to meet.

Index

Websites

Due to the changing nature of Internet links, PowerKids Press has developed an online list of websites related to the subject of this book. This site is updated regularly. Please use this link to access the list: www.powerkidslinks.com/disc/vinci/